Needle Felting: A Beginner's Guide to Creating Simple & Beautiful Needle Felting Projects With Step by Step Instructions & Illustrative Pictures

Jane Macaulay

Copyright@2022

TABLE OF CONTENTS

Chapter 1 3

    INTRODUCTION TO NEEDLE FELTING 4

    The Origin of Needle Felting 8

Chapter 2 9

    NEEDLE FELTING TOOLS AND SUPPLIES 10

    Types of Fiber for Needle Felting 16

Chapter 3 25

    THE FUNDAMENTALS OF NEEDLE FELTING .. 25

    Technique & Tips of Needling 26

Chapter 5 30

    SIMPLE FELTING PROJECTS 30

    Felted Garland 30

    NEEDLE-FELT OWL 38

    Needle Felted Flowers 44

Chapter 1

INTRODUCTION TO NEEDLE FELTING

Needle felting is a craft of using specialized needles to repeatedly poke and prod wool or other types of fibers. Flat felted objects and 2D or 3D sculptures can both be produced using this method. The results of needle felting can be quite lovely, and it's a terrific way to add texture and dimension to your craft item

The general felting process must first be understood in order to comprehend needle felting. Wool fibers are agitated (basically moved back and forth) during felting until a tight bond forms between them. This method uses hot water to make wool felt sheets similar to those you would typically find in craft stores. While the process is mimicked, a needle is used to agitate the material when making needle felt.

For this craft, the kind of needle used is crucial. On the tip of a felting needle are minute barbs that point in a single direction. The bond is formed when the needle is inserted into the wool because the barbs pull the fibers in but not out. You should use a "cushion," which is a thick foam pad that prevents the needles from breaking while also providing you with a stable work surface, because you'll be repeatedly stabbing the fibers.

"Stabbing The Wool" – A Simple Needle Felting Method

The process of pushing the needle into the wool and pulling it out again is known as "stabbing" when it comes to needle felting.

Felting is, in essence, is the act of creating felt, a material created by mixing and compressing loose fibers, such as hair or wool roving.

The hair is simply tangled to create a matted piece.

Do you ever have thick hair tangles that are challenging to comb out? It is similar to felting.

The wool is matted using a particular barbed or notched felting needle in the process of needle felting.

The wool is never wet during the process, as opposed to wet felting, which involves water, detergent, and agitation to cause the wool to get felted.

The term "needle felting" is confusing. It basically involves making a fabric out of wool, such wool roving, using unique, barbed felting needles.

There are numerous ways to needle felt. By felting the wool inside cookie cutters, we will shape these pieces. These wool forms also make amusing tiny Christmas ornaments and can be used as patches or clothing decorations.

The Origin of Needle Felting

Although the history of needle felting is somewhat obscure, it is thought to have started in either Asia or Europe. The process was reportedly first employed to make felt for garments and other products. Tapestries and rugs could have been made with needle felting as well.

In the early 19th century, needle felting was used for the first time to make toys and other items. In the 20th century, needle felting gained popularity when it was used to make sculptures and other works of art.

Today, a variety of things are made with needle felting, including clothes, accessories, toys, and home decor. Most importantly, it is also employed in a number of other crafts, including the creation of jewelry and quilts.

Chapter 2

NEEDLE FELTING TOOLS AND SUPPLIES

You will need the following for needle felting:

- Wool or wool roving
- felting needles
- cookie cutters for making flat shapes.
- a felting pad or a very thick sponge to start this fiber craft. This will shield your lap, the table, and the fragile felting needles from damage.
- Finger guards

You can also get a full felting kit that includes everything you need to get started.

FELTING NEEDLES

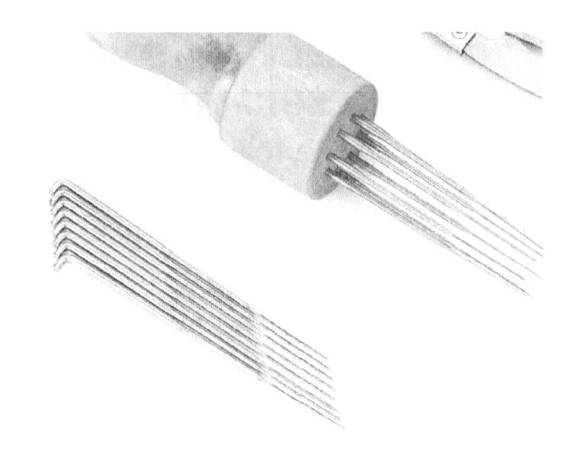

Use a single needle or several, depending on the area you are trying to felt. For instance, felting with a single needle is simpler on smaller surfaces and edges.

The needle's gauge, or diameter, determines how thin it is and how big or little its barbs are. A needle with more barbs will felt faster and more forcefully, but it will also produce a punch hole that is more obvious and may not be as accurate for fine detail work.

Star is a four-sided, aggressive needle felter; more sides equal more barbs.

The spiral is a very aggressive felter, but it shouldn't be used with a mettle armature since the spiral gives the impression that it is much more delicate, and even at a lesser gauge, it tends to break easily. But it's still my preferred needle. When you use it, it has a smooth sensation.

Three-sided triangles have strong needles; fewer sides also mean fewer barbs. For finer work, a triangular needle with a gauge of 42 could be better because it has fewer barbs. excellent for eyesight.

A crown needle and a forked needle are also present. They appear to be the doll producers' go-to tools for adding hair to the dolls.

The lanolin (natural oils) in the wool will prevent rusting, and as an added bonus, storing your needles in a pepper shaker with some raw fiber in the bottom will keep them accessible and orderly.

Wool or Wool Roving

Roving wool

Core Wool

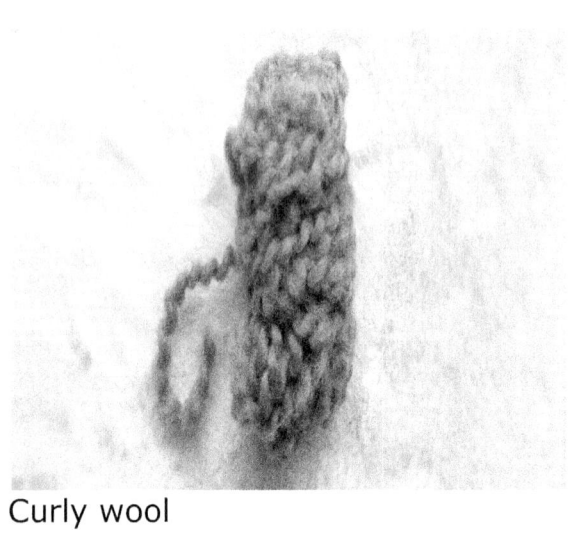

Curly wool

The demand for wool or roving follows. This can take the shape of fine mohair, raw sheep wool, or alpaca fiber. You are completely in control.

I advise you to get wool roving if you're just starting off with felting. This roving is prewashed, and you can buy multipacks of it that are filled with gorgeous colors. This will prevent you from having a large quantity of wool in just one color.

Types of Fiber for Needle Felting

Alpaca

Alpaca fiber is unquestionably the best in the world! Alpaca is suitable for needle felting but is slightly hairier (soft hairy not course hairy). Because it is too fine, it is not ideal for sculpting or making dense items.

 It works best on small surfaces like detailed fiber painting, where you use tiny bits of each color you need, for making felted animal pelts, for example.

Additionally it is fantastic for doll hair, horse or lion manes.

Corriedale Sliver

It felts quickly and works well to create dense, substantial sculptures.

Core Fiber

This is a Sheep wool that typically has a coarser, shorter staple. It is great for sculpting the core.

Combed -Top

An example is the Merino sheep. is which are better for wet felting. When needle felted, stable is too long, leaves punch marks, and has a stringy, unfinished appearance. However, it can be used very effectively to give something long hair for example, to do hairy patch on a cat's cheek.

Decorative Bits

For effect, sparkle, and texture in your needle felting projects, you can also add Mohair curls, Firestar, Angelina, Bamboo, or other silky cellulose fibers.

- **Felting Pad**

A felting pad is basically a thought piece of soft material which has two major purposes.

A felting pad firstly safeguards the surface beneath the wool, be it a table or your lap. Second, it provides something soft for the felting needles to stick into so they won't shatter.

You may also use a substantial sponge, such as one you can find in an auto or hardware store, for this purpose. Although they are inexpensive and simple to locate, the negative is that after multiple uses, those sponges don't hold up very well.

Consequently, I advise utilizing a felting pad if you plan to make numerous needle felted items. You should be able to find one at a craft store or your neighborhood yarn store, and they last a lot longer.

Other felting Supplies include

- Scissors for cutting and boring holes

- Craft Wire: They are used to make felted animals bendable, for example on their arms and legs.

- Glue: It is used to attach any embellishments such as eyes and nose on a felted creatures.

FeltIng Surfaces

- **Felting Pad**

There are several possibilities for a felting pad. A chair cushion's material can alternatively be bought from a fabric store and trimmed to size with an electric knife. However, because this cushion is typically not as substantial, it will quickly fail, either by leaving noticeable divots or by breaking off and falling into your project. In a pinch, it does function, though.

- **Rice Bag**

This is done using a burlap rectangle. Its numerous layers sewn together, leaving a corner open for a funnel. Utilizing the funnel, stuff bag with rice and fix the corner. For each project, you may replace the bag's top with a fresh piece of burlap, and you can attach it to your pad with quilting clips.

Instead of making one from scratch, you might be able to locate a drawstring burlap bag; however, multiple bags would work best because one layer is actually insufficient.

- **Felting Chunky**

This is a felted square or rectangle that has been felted so tightly that nothing can felt to it anymore but can still be plied with needles.

Chapter 3

THE FUNDAMENTALS OF NEEDLE FELTING

The following are the basic steps involved in needle felting with which you can use to create any object of your choice.

1. Assemble the materials: wool, felting needles, cookie cutters, a pad, and finger guards.

2. Spread the wool out thinly and use a cookie cutter.

3. Insert a felting needle into the wool, then remove it. Repeat along the edges and all over the fiber.

4. Flip the wool over and perform Step 3 again.

5. Continue felting the wool until it becomes a piece of fabric that cannot be separated.

Technique & Tips of Needling

- Keep your eyes on your project at all times during needling.
- Always poke or stab straight down. Do not puncture the needle and then tilt it.
- Deep Needling: To alter the felt's form and density, punch down firmly and directly.
- Surface needling - To add colors without altering shape,

gently poke just through the topmost layer.
- Deep Line Needling: By repeatedly stabbing along the same route or in the same location, a depression or crevice will form, which can be utilized to add depth or definition. Before poking, the fiber can be gently guided into position with a needle.
- Flat Felting: Lay out the necessary layers of fibers across the felting surface, then needle the entire thing. Pick up the fiber with care, then flip it over to needle the other side. Do this often until your fiber becomes dense,

smooth, and less likely to stick to the sponge.

- Making a good edge on flat felt: Repeatedly needling the same line will give your felt a nice edge. The narrower edge should be folded over the line and needle. If you want to make a "fat lip edge," place a needle immediately behind the fold and roll, fold, and place a needle behind fold repeatedly until you achieve the desired thickness.
- Felted Ball or Log: To begin a dense ball, tie a few knots in roving. Fold the fiber over the knots and sew it with a needle, rotating it constantly

to sew both sides. You can start by tightly wrapping fiber around a dowel, toothpick, or skewer before rolling it into a log with your hands. Until you reach the correct thickness, keep adding fiber. Remove the dowel and needle, then roll the pad over the edges until they are smooth. To thoroughly smooth it out, roll it in your hand.

- Thin felted string: To make a tight string, pull a very little piece of fiber and roll it on a sponge or moisten your fingers and roll it on a flat surface.

Chapter 5

SIMPLE FELTING PROJECTS

Felted Garland

Materials Needed

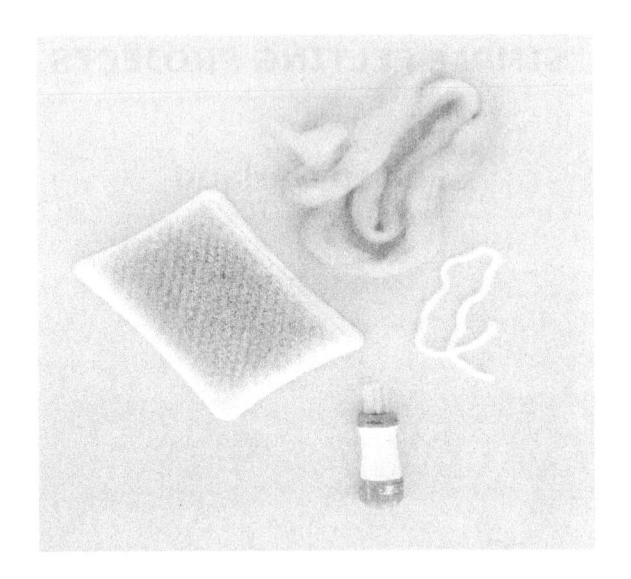

- Wool roving- Use 1 ounce to make two 1inches macarons to get enough for your garland in any colors you like.
- Felting mat or pad
- Felting needle
- White roving yarn

- Baking twine
- Embroidery needle

Instructions

Step 1: To start, cut a piece of colored roving that is 48 inches long. Spread the roving out to let the fibers loosen up a bit and flatten it out a bit rather than keeping it in a strand.

Step 2: Form a tight ball out of the roving. While rolling it up, you should change the direction of the roving to make it more resemble a uniform ball rather than a cinnamon roll. If it has lumps or is a little off-center, don't worry; the needle felting will even it out.

Step 3: Set the ball of roving on your felting mat and repeatedly prick it with the needle tool. The roving will begin to bind together as you do this to form a sturdy ball-shaped piece.

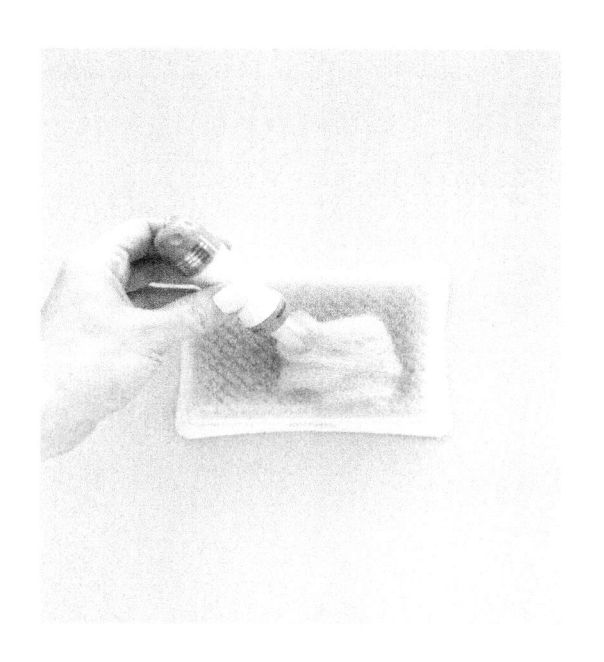

Use the needles to prick the roving into a disc-like macaron shape since we are making them.

Remember to flip the object over and feel it from all angles.

Step 4: After you've cut it into a macaron shape, tie a 6" piece of white roving yarn around the middle to make the "filling." Then use the needles to prick this roving yarn to felt it onto the macaron. Trim the extra yarn after the two pieces have been felted together.

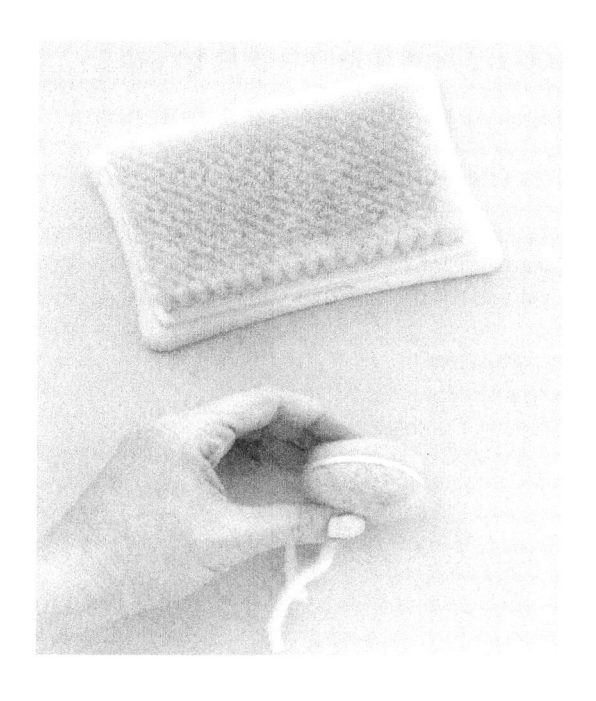

Step 5: Continue making macarons in the same manner with each of your roving colors. They come together fairly quickly once you get the hang of it. Each macaron will take you between five and ten minutes to make.

Step 6: The final step is to stitch through the top of each macaron with the baker's twine threaded onto an embroidery needle to form a garland.

It is ready to hang once you tie off the ends.

NEEDLE-FELT OWL

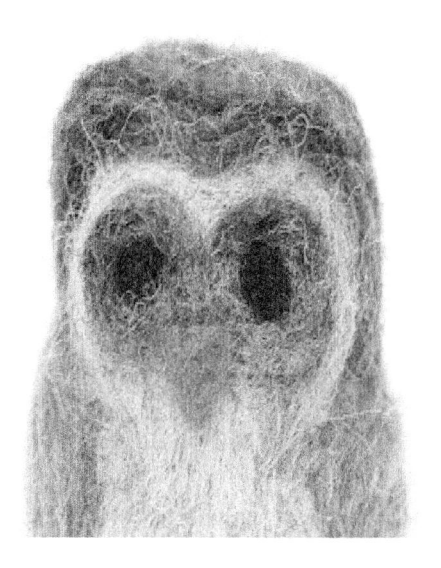

Materials needed:

• Wool batting for the core or cream-colored roving

- 5 colors of wool roving in the hues of your choice for owls

- 36 or 38 gauge felting needle(s)

- Scissors

Instructions

1. Take a handful of the wool batting and roll it into a ball between your palms. Now shape the ball with a needle into an oval.

We want to be able to still attach more wool to it, so don't needle it too tightly. To enable the owl to stand up without rolling over, needle one small end flat next. You now possess the owl's foundation.

Take a few wisps of your lightest color at this point. Layer the wisps over your owl base and needle it until attached.

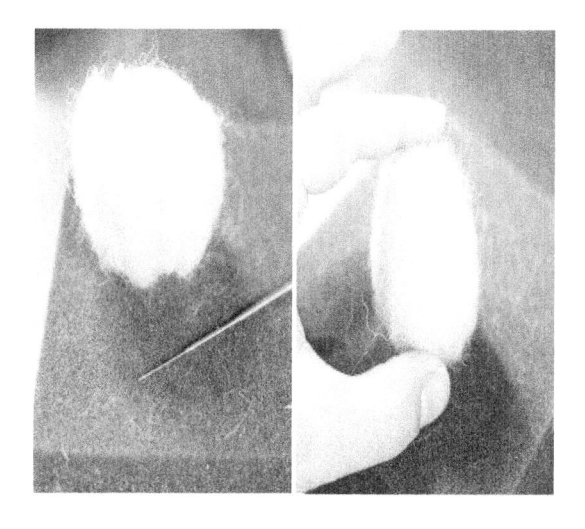

2. Grab a few wisps of your second color and needle it over the top and sides of your owl.

At this point, work the area with your needle until you are happy with the indent to add a little definition to where the owl's head and wings meet.

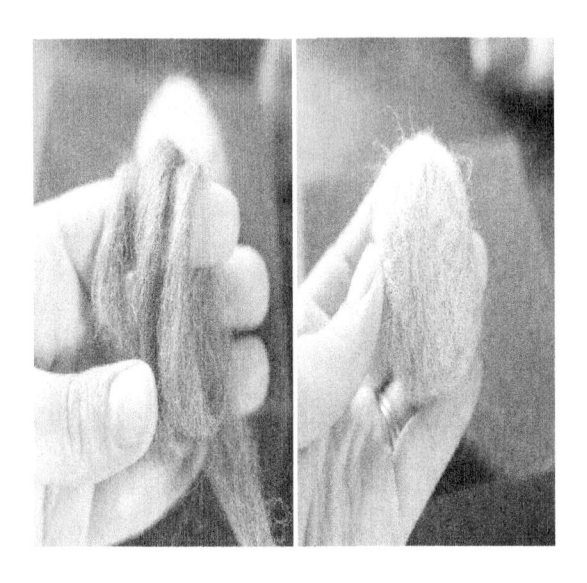

3. Take a tiny bit of your final color and delicately needle it around the owl's face. With the wool, create tiny peaks to resemble ears.

We will now focus on the face's finer details.

5. Pick up a tiny bit of your owl color and needle it onto the face to create two interconnected circles.

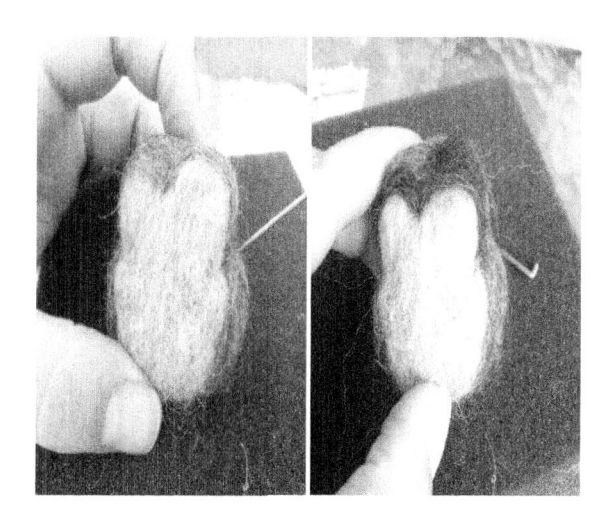

Next, pierce a tiny piece of black wool into the centers of the pupil-shaped circles you just created. Last but not least, create the beak by needling a tiny piece of orange wool into an upside-down triangle shape.

You are done!

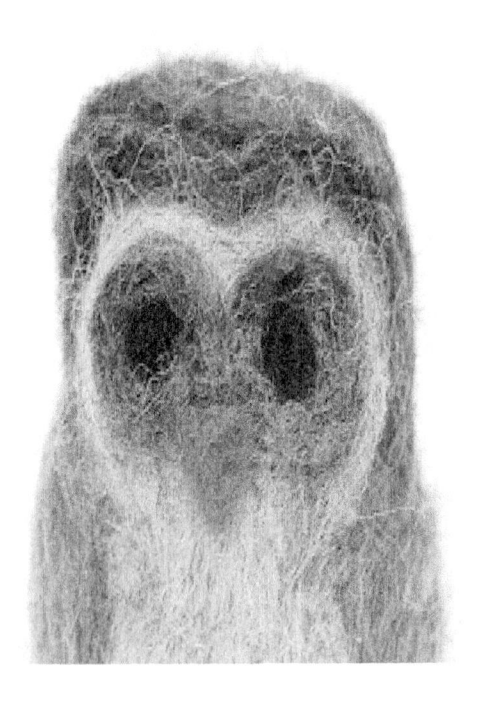

I hope you adore it as much as I do.

Needle Felted Flowers

Materials Needed

- Pure wool yarn that has been shredded, roving, or wool tops.

- Needles for felting. Many needle felters start with thicker felting needles before gradually narrowing them down so that the holes get smaller as the piece is finished. I usually only use a size 38 triangular needle, but I start out by using 4 or 5. I then scale it back until I'm using just 1 needle to complete the final sculpting.

• A felting brush or thick foam to apply the felt.

• While carders and wool combs are optional, they do aid in blending colors and separating fibers prior to starting the felting process.

• Cutter shape. For this project, the sugar flower cutter is used because it's sturdy and has a plastic ridge I can grip.

Instructions

1. You must first get your fibers ready for felting by simply separating the fibers with your hands will aid in the felting procedure. Combine two colors to create a more vibrant look.

Instead of using a cookie cutter, a sugar flower cutter is being used because it's slightly more comfortable to hold and because the extra circle around the base of the cutter keeps your fingers a little further away from the sharp felting needles.

2. Fill the cutter with your combed fibers, making sure they all pass through the center to firmly attach all the petals. With practice, it is possible to create finished flowers with darker centers and lighter outer petals (or vice versa)
3. Once all the fibers have reduced and are only filling the cutter's bottom, take your felting needles and simply keep poking around inside the cutter.

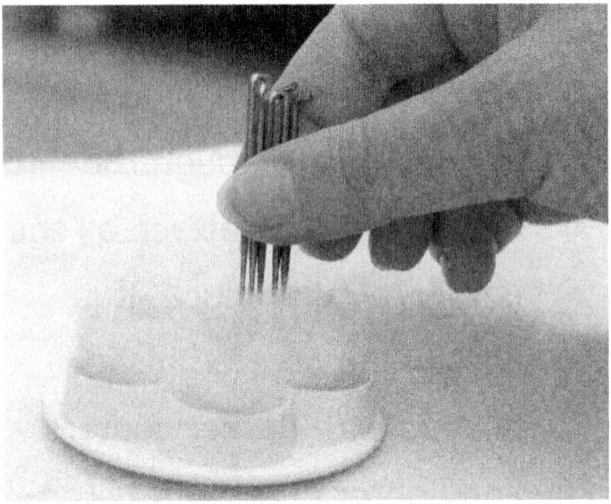

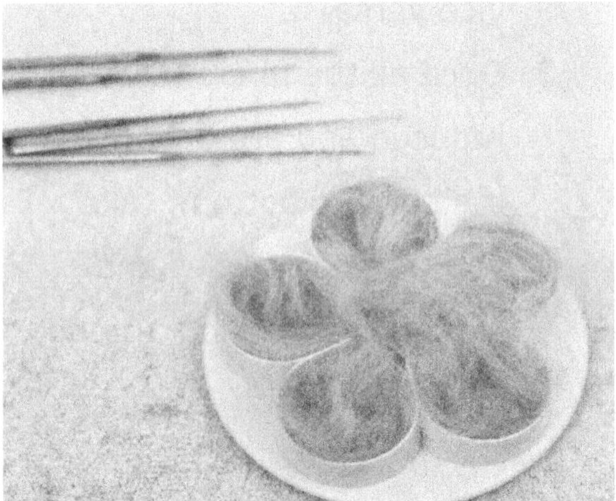

The edges of the felting needle have teeny tiny barbs, which cause the fibers to tangle and compact with each insertion. Your wool will get denser as you stab and prod it, and it will shrink or felt more.

When the flower appears to be quite compacted at the base of the cutter, turning it and going through the felting process again helps to create a nice dense flower. With each turn, the flower in this illustration becomes feltier.

It was time to advance to the next phase by the conclusion of the fourth stabbing.

This method combines three steps into one: coloring the petals further, making a flower's center, and felting the petals even more. For the remainder of the flower, you can use only one needle.

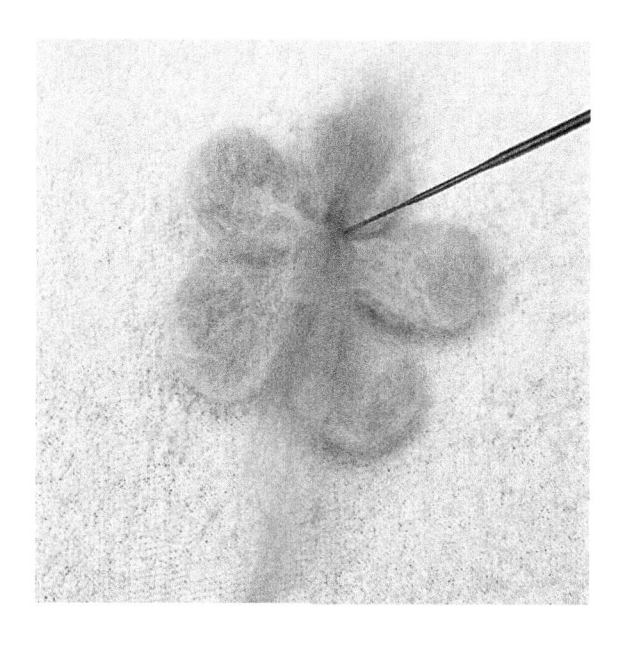

Lay a tiny wisp of fibers in a contrasting color over one of the petals after removing it. I usually position it so that the length of the petal I want to work on is just past one end of it.

When there is no more contrasting fiber to secure into the petal, stop inserting the needle into the petal.

Start at the base of the petal and gradually work your way up.

As you go around each petal, add a light coating of color and then needle the remaining material into the center. Continue to work on the center until it is quite dense with hardly any fibers protruding.

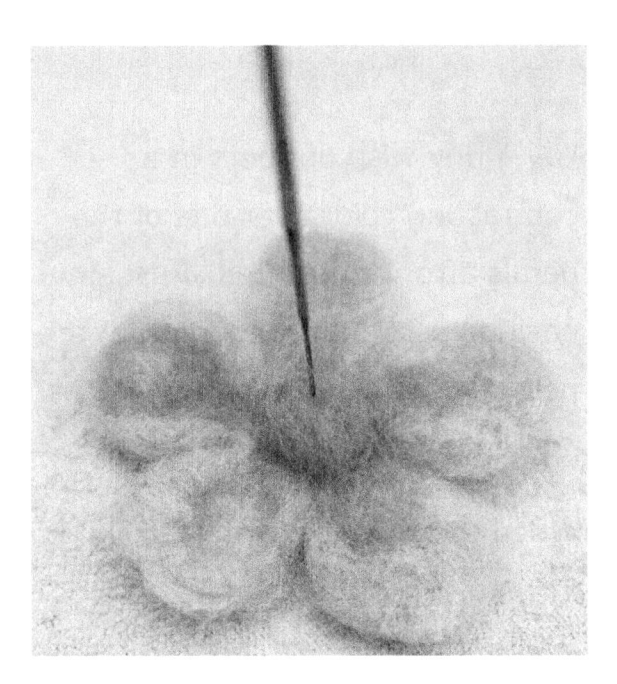

Once the center is complete, the flower simply needs to be neatened around the edges to remove any remaining fuzziness. I usually accomplish this by lifting the stray fibers with the tip of my needle and almost "folding" them in.

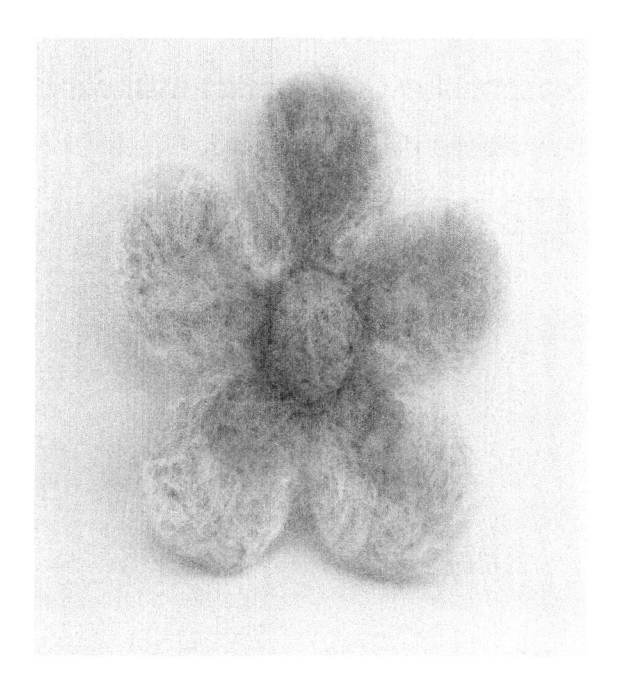

Everyone has a different needle felting style, and the process is not exactly scientific. While some people leave their pieces quite loose, others continue to work on them until they are very solid and dense.

You should continue poking and prodding it until it feels like a reasonably sturdy object with very few fibers protruding but is still fairly soft and squashy.

How lovely they are.

You can attach them to a straw and put in a flower vase. You can also use them to design a head band.

.

Printed in Great Britain
by Amazon